This Book Belongs To Me!

(Write your name below)

____

You can think of this book as your **friend**—someone who's here to help you
Learn, Stay safe, and Grow stronger every day.
Take care of your book, and it'll always be here for you when you need it.

Growing Up Strong

Your Body Safety Checklist

SANDRA K ANIL

Copyright © <2025> <Sandra K Anil>

Made with ❤ on the Notion Press Platform

www.notionpress.com

To the love of my life, my first kids, Vishal Krishna and Vedhika; to my beloved grandparents; to my lovely family; to my inspiring teachers; and to the family I have chosen along the way.

Contents

Foreword

As we watch our children grow and flourish, we as parents want to equip them with the knowledge, confidence, and resilience to navigate the world safely and happily. "Growing Up Strong" is a remarkable resource that does just that. This book not only teaches children about body safety but also gently guides them in understanding and managing their emotions, recognizing their strengths, and developing a positive self-image - essential life skills that will benefit them for years to come.

Sandra has poured her heart and soul into creating a book that is not just informative but engaging and creative too. Through colourful illustrations and relatable cartoons, she gently guides young readers through the process of identifying their body parts and understanding the importance of body safety.

I must confess that I have always been deeply inspired by Sandra's efforts to make a positive impact on the lives of people. Her passion, dedication, and commitment to empowering young minds are qualities that I have always admired. I have no doubt that she is destined for great things, and "Growing Up Strong" is just the beginning. This book is a testament to her unwavering commitment to creating a safer, more supportive world for children, and I am sure that it will be a stepping stone to even greater accomplishments.

To Sandra, I offer my heartfelt appreciation for this outstanding contribution to the field of child safety and education. Your work will undoubtedly make a profound difference in the lives of countless children, and for that, we are all deeply grateful.

To the young readers of this book, I say: remember that you are strong, capable, and deserving of respect and kindness. Never hesitate to speak up, to ask for help, or to trust your instincts. You are the future leaders, change-makers, and heroes of our world, and I have no doubt that you will grow up to be brave, wise, and compassionate individuals.

Kavitha Shyam Sreedhar

Psychologist & Clinical Hypnotherapist

10-02-2025

Preface

To be born in this wonderful world is a gift, and living in it is a great opportunity to explore its vast beauty. However, as responsible humans, it is our duty to ensure that everyone, especially our children, is provided with a space to live a happy and healthy life. Unfortunately, challenges like abuse, particularly child sexual abuse, fill our hearts with fear and anxiety.

As per the National Crime Records Bureau (NCRB) of India, crimes against children increased by 8.7% in 2022 compared to the previous year. A total of 1,62,449 cases were registered, with significant crimes reported under Kidnapping & Abduction (45.7%) and the Protection of Children from Sexual Offences Act (POCSO), 2012, which accounted for 39.7%, including cases of child rape.

MentX, my entrepreneurial venture aimed at sexual abuse prevention and mental health awareness, was founded in 2019 under the campaign "Mission Her." This initiative began as a protest against the delay in justice and the rising incidents of rape in the country. From its inception, MentX, then known as Mission Her, has had a volunteer team of 50 members and has implemented various initiatives to raise awareness around abuse prevention.

What started as a simple protest soon evolved into a realization of the critical role that comprehensive sexuality education (CSE) plays in addressing this issue. Since then, MentX has focused on providing age-appropriate comprehensive sexuality education to all. Though our work is primarily centered in Kerala, we aspire to expand across the country.

The idea for MentX came to me during my college days in 2019. While I graduated with a degree in B.Tech Naval Architecture and Shipbuilding, I felt called to serve a different purpose. Alongside my professional career, I began conducting awareness programs for MentX. However, my background in engineering posed challenges in my role as a Comprehensive Sexuality Educator.

To address these challenges, I immersed myself in learning, reading everything I could on the subject and collaborating with health professionals and psychologists such as Dr. Lissy Shajahan (Celebrity Life Coach, Psychologist, and Author), Dr. Sania Siddiqui (Founder of the Humjoli Foundation - Thane), and Dr. Ankit Chandra (Author of "The Complete Guide on Sex Education"). Through my collaboration with Dr. Ankit, MentX's volunteer team translated his book into Malayalam, marking MentX's first publication.

I also completed TARSHI's eLearning course on Comprehensive Sexuality Education for Teachers and Educators in 2021, which greatly enhanced the effectiveness of MentX's sessions. (Talking About Reproductive and Sexual Health Issues – TARSHI, is an NGO based in New Delhi). Additionally, Nilima Achwal from Iesha Learning (This initiative has developed India's first comprehensive sexuality and gender education digital toolkit for teachers) helped me during the initial stages of MentX. I further deepened my understanding by completing a certificate course on Menstrual Health and Hygiene Management (MHHM) from the Humjoli Foundation under Dr. Sania Siddiqui, who continues to guide me in delivering MHHM sessions. Currently, I am pursuing my Master's in Psychology from Indira Gandhi Open University to strengthen my ability to serve in this field.

Since 2019, I have been facilitating age-appropriate Comprehensive Sexuality Education sessions for school children. However, one key lesson I've learned is that a single 2-hour session in high school is insufficient to equip children with the knowledge to navigate a safe and healthy life. CSE must follow a developmental approach, starting from learning body part names at the toddler stage and advancing through the stages of a child's development. The topics should cover all aspects of human sexual health by the time they reach adulthood. It is also critical that these concepts be revisited regularly to reinforce them in children's minds.

This realization led to the creation of this book, which serves as a medium for children aged 10-12 years to learn about body safety and revise the topics at their own pace until they are firmly ingrained in their minds. Although there are many books available on similar topics, access to them may be limited, and cultural differences may influence how the material is presented. "Growing Up Strong" has been written with Indian children in mind and tailored to suit their learning style. This book can be used as a guide for parents and educators to address these essential topics with children. Future versions of this book for other age groups, as well as books specifically for parents and educators, will be released by MentX.

The ultimate purpose of this book is to create a safer world for our children—a world where they can live, learn, and play fearlessly and holistically.

Sandra K Anil

Author, Educator & Founder - MentX

19-01-2025

Acknowledgments

I extend my heartfelt gratitude to my mentor, Dr. Lissy Shajahan, Celebrity Life Coach, Psychologist, and Author, who has been a guiding light in both my professional and personal life. The immense confidence she has instilled in me is invaluable.

To Malavika K J, my beloved sister, who beautifully designed the cover page of this book and brought its essence to life.

To my dearest Kavitha Shyam Sreedhar, Psychologist & Clinical Hypnotherapist, who graciously penned the foreword and has always been a sisterly figure to me.

To Dr. Ankit Chandra, Community Physician, Researcher, and Author, for his invaluable guidance on comprehensive sexuality education.

To Devipriya K, Co-founder of MentX and my best friend since childhood, without whom MentX would never have been possible.

To the incredible volunteers of MentX, my entrepreneurial venture dedicated to sexual abuse prevention and mental health awareness. Your unwavering commitment and passion for this mission inspire me every day.

And to my partner, Yedu Krishna K J, for being my unwavering cheerleader, constructive critic, and greatest admirer.

Lastly, a heartfelt thank you to the universe for its endless blessings and for leading me on this incredible journey. Every twist and turn has been a part of the larger plan, and I am deeply grateful for the guidance and energy that continues to surround me.

Each of you has played a unique and irreplaceable role in this journey, and I am deeply grateful for your support and encouragement.

Introduction

"Hello, friends! I am **Minty**. You can think of me as your elder sister and a proud member of the **MentX Super Squad.** First of all, congratulations on choosing this book! Let me tell you what's inside and how it can help you. I'll be with you every step of the way, making this reading journey fun and enjoyable.

This book carries some very important messages to help you stay safe and healthy. You are blessed with a wonderful and unique body. It's something to be thankful for, and it's your responsibility to keep it protected and happy. But to do that, you need to learn a few important things.

In this book, we'll be reading together about:

- Your amazing body and its special parts

- The changes your body goes through as you grow up

- What is good and bad for your body

- What to do if something bad happens

- How to get help when you need it

MentX Super Squad is a group that is aware of above things and shares them with other children to help them stay safe.

To make reading even more fun, there are activities like fill-in-the-blanks, coloring, crosswords, and much more! Remember, if you have any doubts or questions, don't hesitate to ask your parents or teachers—they're here to help you. By the time you finish this book, you'll know all the **Body Safety Rules to protect yourself**. Oh, and guess what? There's a special bonus waiting for you at the end! But no peeking—read through the book first to unlock it.

Are you ready to start this exciting journey of learning? Let's go!"

1. My Body Is Mine

Minty: " Hey! Imagine you're taking notes from the blackboard, and suddenly your pen stops working. What would you do then?"

Minty: "Usually, we ask for permission before taking something that belongs to another person because that thing is **OWNED** by them. Can you think of some things you have that belong to you? Things that are really special to you? List five things you own here:"

-
-
-
-
-

Minty: " I'm glad to know you own these things. Now, have you ever thought about your body this way? It helps you learn, play, and live. Isn't it something really special to you? So, who owns your body? Is it your parents or someone else?"

Minty: " Your body belongs to you. Yes, **you are the owner of your body**! Just like asking for permission before taking someone's pen, your ownership of your body works the same way. If the pen's owner says no, you shouldn't force them to give it to you—you respect their choice. In the same way, you have the full **POWER** to decide what happens to your body."

"Wait! Did you see these pictures? Can you identify what these people are doing?"

Minty: "Exactly! You do similar things too, right? Imagine your parent hugging you, or your friend holding your hand. Or maybe you can recall a moment when your parents asked you to give a kiss to your sibling. These are some ways people interact with each other to show love and care. But remember, you are the owner of your body. If you don't feel like hugging or doing something similar, it is **OK to say no.** Your feelings and choices about your body are important, and others should respect them."

"Is this question popping into your mind? What if they are bigger than you? What if they are older than you? What if they seem friendly or act nicely?"

"Whoever the person is—no matter their age or how friendly they seem— if they ask you to do something to your body that feels wrong or makes you uncomfortable, **YOU SHOULD SAY NO.** Say it loudly and clearly. Repeat it until they stop or hear you. And if they still don't stop, **it's OK to SCREAM TOO!"**

Minty: "Remember, just like your body belongs to you and you have the full power to decide what happens to it, the same goes for others. If someone doesn't want you to hug them or even shake hands, you should respect their choice. You should never force them to do something they don't want to do. It's important to always ask for permission before doing anything involving another person. This act is called **CONSENT.** Now, may I ask you one more question? Is your body beautiful?

____

____

Minty: "What makes a body beautiful? Do you ever feel jealous of someone because you think they're more beautiful than you?"

____

____

Minty: "You see, everything in this world is beautiful. Our bodies might differ in size, shape, or even color, but that doesn't mean one body is more beautiful than another. Whether tall or short, thin or curvy, dark or fair—every body is unique and beautiful. We are all equally beautiful. Just like we all have favorite colors or toys, some people might like a particular shape or color more, but that's just their personal choice. It doesn't make anyone else less attractive. Did you get that? If so, say it with me:"

'I AM BEAUTIFUL. EVERYONE IS BEAUTIFUL. WE ARE ALL EQUALLY BEAUTIFUL!'

Minty: "Perfect! Now, let me share one more secret with you. Do you know what makes this world so amazing?

____

____

Minty: "It's the differences between everything! Imagine if all living things looked the same, if there was only one type of fruit, or if the entire world had just one color. Wouldn't that be so boring? It's these differences that make the world so wonderful and exciting. **So, if you ever feel like you're different, remember this: you're adding more beauty to the world!** Be proud of this amazing gift you're giving to everyone."

Hey! How was your chit-chat with Minty? What did you learn from her?

____

____

That's great! Minty was telling you that you are the owner of your body and that you have the full power to decide what happens to it.

Now, look at the next page. There's a beautiful picture waiting for you to add some colors to it!"

2. Naming My Body Parts

Minty: "Hello, friends! Did you color the picture? I'm sure you did an amazing job. Now, can I take a peek into your pencil box? What do you have inside it? List them below:"

-
-
-
-
-

Minty: "You know exactly what's inside your pencil box because you're the boss of it, right? In the same way, it's important to know about the parts of your body since you're the owner of it. Hmm… let me check if you can identify the parts in the pictures below!"

Minty: "Well done! You already know most of the body parts, which you learn at a very young age. You probably even know how these parts help you. But many children your age might not know the names of the genital parts between their legs. Let me tell you: for boys, this part is called the **PENIS.** For girls, it's called the **VULVA.** They are also known as private parts.

The penis helps boys pass urine and, when they grow up, it also plays a role in making babies. Don't worry—you'll learn more about that when you're a bit older. For girls, an opening called urethra near to vulva region helps in passing urine and the vulva helps in making babies when they grow up. Now, can you write the names of the parts between the legs of a boy and a girl here?"

____

____

Minty: "Awesome! Now I've got something to help you summarize what we just talked about. "

Body Parts	Functions
Eyes	See, Observe
Ears	Hear, Listen
Nose	Smell, Breath
Legs	Walk, Run
Hands	Hold, Grab
Penis (Boys)	Urinate, Reproduce
Urethra (Girls)	Urinate
Vulva (Girls)	Reproduce

Minty: "Did you find that helpful? Using the right names for all body parts is very important. If your vulva or penis hurts and you don't know what to call it, it can be difficult to

explain and get help. You might have nicknames for these parts, but the person you talk to might not understand them. That's why it's so important to learn the correct names. *And voila! See you again soon. Bye!"*

3. My Growing Body

Minty: "Hey, how are you? I'm so excited! I'm going to meet my cousin's new baby today. I can't wait to see the little one! Do you have any younger siblings or cousins?"

____

____

Minty: "You know, I always wonder how a baby's body is so different from ours. Look at how your body is different from younger kids or older adults. Your size, height, and weight all change, right? What do you think that means?"

____

____

Minty: "Yes, that means our bodies are constantly changing! Our height, weight, and size keep growing and changing. As our physical bodies change, our internal organs and their functions also change with age. Between the ages of 8 and 13, a lot of changes happen to your body. This growing period is called..."

To find out the answer, color the pictures below!

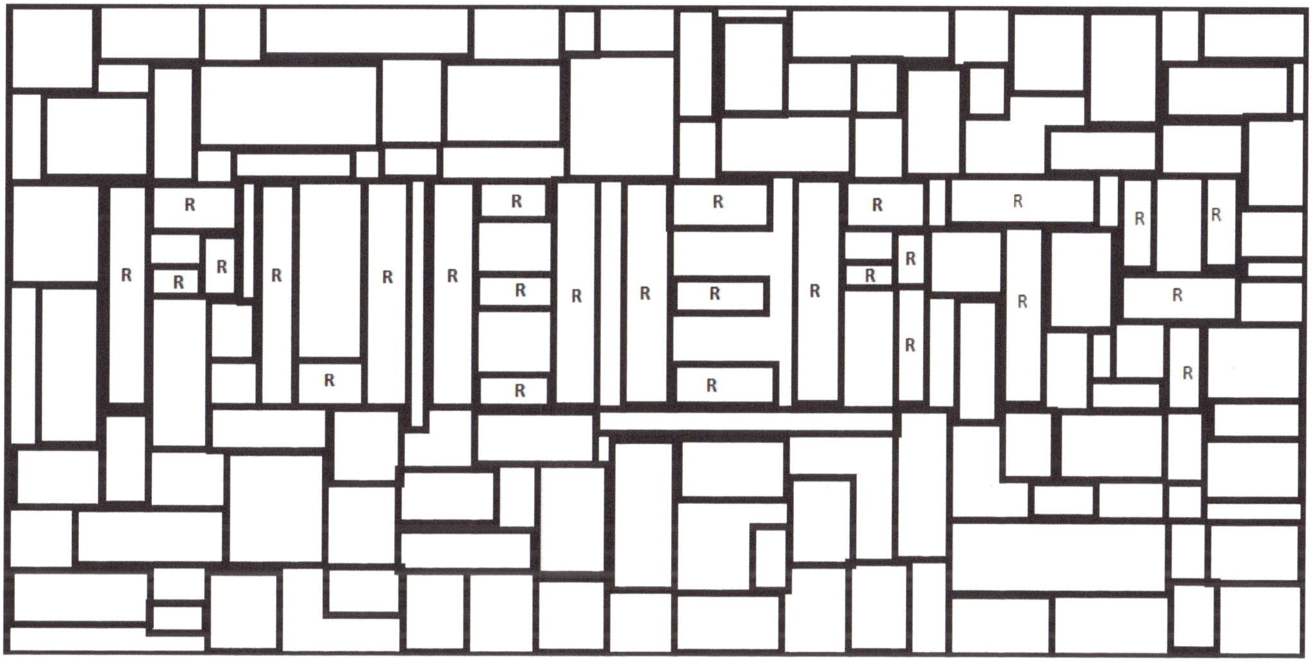

Instruction: Color the grids marked "R" in red. Use any color of your choice for the remaining grids.

Minty: "That's right! The growing period is called puberty. Can you identify some of the changes happening to your body?"

____

____

____

____

Minty: "To help you with that, I've written a fun song. Check it out below!"

The Puberty Song

Step by step, you're growing tall,
Puberty's here—it's part of it all!
For boys, your voice will start to crack,
You'll grow some hair on your face and back!

For girls, your hips will widen, too,
Breasts will grow—it's all brand new!
Periods come, it's nothing strange,
It's just your body starting to change!

Step by step, you're on your way,
Growing stronger every day,
No need to rush, enjoy the ride,
You're becoming you, with pride

Minty: "I hope you liked the song! Before I go, there's something important to talk about."

Wet Dreams and Erections (For Boys):

"As boys grow, the penis, which helped you urinate when you were younger, now has other jobs. Sometimes, when you see something romantic or even just out of nowhere, your penis can become **erect (hard).** This happens when blood rushes to the area. It can also happen when you're feeling good or happy about yourself. Sometimes, it may happen in the morning, too. This is completely normal."

"Additionally, sometimes a white fluid (semen) may come out of the penis instead of urine. This can happen while you are sleeping, and it's called a **'wet dream' or 'nightfall.'** It's a normal part of growing up and nothing to worry about."

Menstruation (For Girls):

"You might know that when a woman is expecting a baby, it grows inside her body for about nine months. The baby stays in an area called the uterus. To feed the baby while it's in the uterus, it gets nutrients from a special lining called the endometrium."

"But before girls can have babies, their bodies go through changes. When a girl becomes mature, her body prepares for a baby, but since we only choose to have babies when we're older, the preparation inside the uterus is removed from the body through the vulva as blood. This is known as a **period (menstruation),** and it can last anywhere from 4 to 7 days. Some girls start their periods earlier, while others may take more time. If you haven't started your period by the age of 15, it's a good idea to see a doctor."

"**The area between legs of girls has three openings:** one for urine (the urethra), one for menstrual blood (the vagina), and one for waste elimination (the anus). The external part of vagina is called **VULVA**"

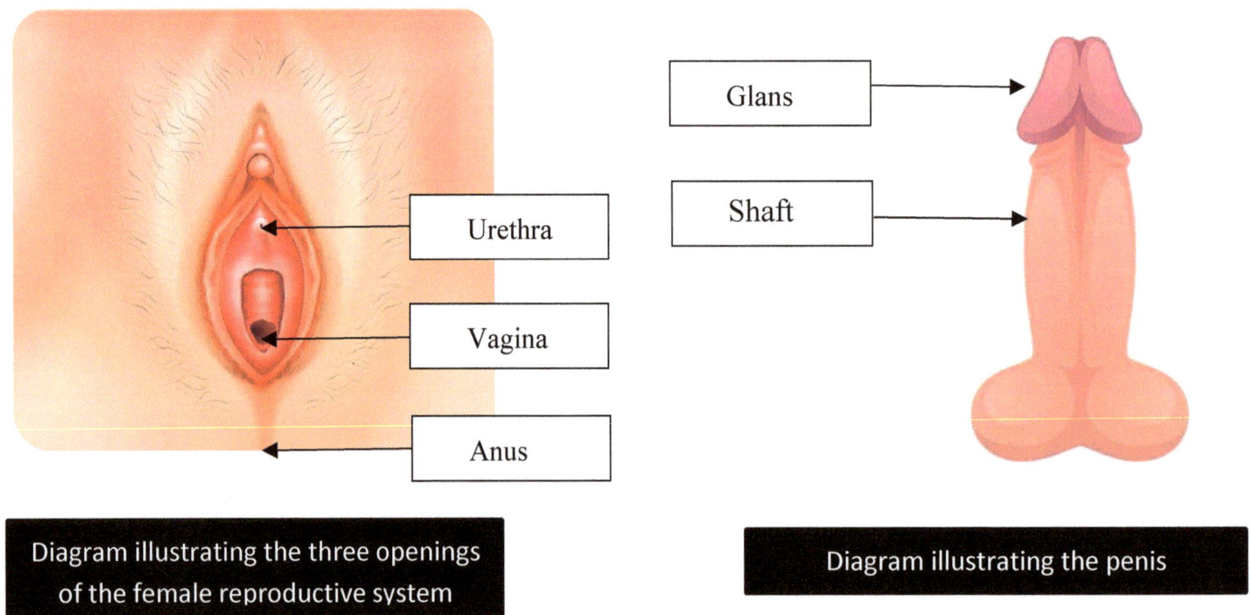

Diagram illustrating the three openings of the female reproductive system

Diagram illustrating the penis

Minty: "And there you are. I'll be back soon with more fun activities. But now, I'm going to visit the baby!

4. Keeping My Body Clean

Minty: "Hey friends! Did you know I visited my baby cousin yesterday? I felt so happy! When I arrived, the baby was being bathed, and it was such a nice thing to see. Do you bathe on your own, or do your parents help you?"

____

____

Minty: "Great! When we're kids, our parents help us bathe and dress, but as we grow, we learn to do it on our own. Now tell me, why do we bathe?"

____

____

Minty: "Exactly! We bathe every day to keep our bodies healthy and clean. Take a look at the pictures given in next page to see how to maintain good hygiene and keep your body fresh."

Bath daily

Brush twice daily

Trim nails regularly

Wear clean clothes

Wash hands properly

Cover sneezes, coughs

Change underwear daily

Wipe & flush after use

Drink more water

Eat healthy food

Sleep enough hours

Stay active daily

Minty: "Hey, there's something important I want to share about boys and girls. When boys grow up, a thin membrane called the foreskin, which covers the tip of the penis, becomes movable. A white fluid called **smegma** can collect under the foreskin, and it's important to clean this area gently with plain water during bathing. Are you following me so far?"

____

____

Minty: "For girls, extra care is needed during periods when menstrual blood flows. You can absorb the blood using a clean cloth or a sanitary pad. It's important to change the pad and replace it with a fresh one every four hours. A sanitary pad will be sticked to your under wear as given in the picture. Once you've used a pad, fold it neatly, wrap it in newspaper or the wrapper that comes with the sanitary pad, and dispose of it in the correct dustbin. Ask your parents or teachers which bin to use, as sanitary pads should not be mixed with other waste. Disposing of them properly ensures waste pickers won't have trouble handling them. Got it?"

____

____

Minty: "Great! Oh, by the way, I'm expecting my period tomorrow. Did you know periods typically repeat every 21–35 days? Tracking this will help you predict when your next period might come. It's normal to miss your period occasionally at a young age, but it's a good idea to visit a doctor if you miss it often or feel unsure about anything. Oops, I'm running late for the medical store! Bye for now!"

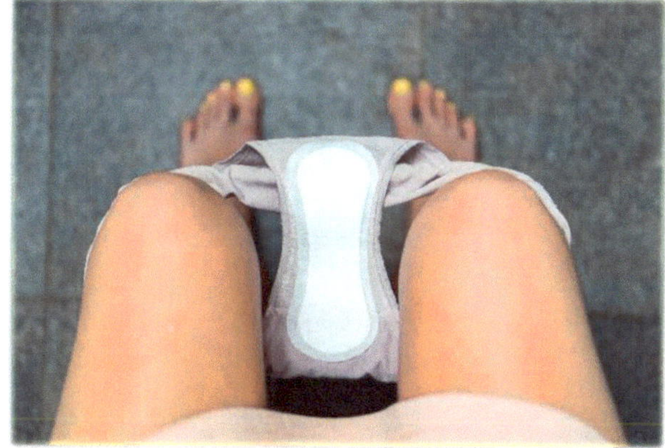

5. Knowing My Feelings

Minty: "Hi friends! I've been having a troubling week lately. I didn't know why, but I was feeling angry and irritable. Then, to my surprise, my Aunt Ziva came to visit. I told her how I was feeling, and she helped me understand it. Do you want to know what she said?"

____

____

Minty: "She explained that our feelings are natural responses to situations or how we experience a particular moment. Everyone has feelings, and they are an important part of being human. Feelings help us share our thoughts and emotions with others, make decisions, and take care of ourselves. Now, take a look at these pictures to understand more!"

Communicating Feelings:

Friend: "You seem upset. Do you want to talk about it?"
You: "Yes, I'm feeling a bit sad because I didn't do well in my test, and I just need someone to listen."

Making Decisions:
Parent: "Do you want to join the football team or the painting club?"
You: "I think I'll choose painting because it makes me feel calm and happy."

Taking Care of Yourself:
Friend: "Want to stay up late and watch another movie?"
You: "No, I'm feeling really tired, so I'll go to bed now to take care of myself.

Minty: "You know, there are positive feelings and negative feelings. Here are some examples:"

Positive Feelings	Negative Feelings
Happy	Angry
Excited	Sad
Proud	Dissapointed
Grateful	Worried
Calm	Hurt
Loved	Guilty
Motivated	Ashamed

Minty: "Sometimes, you might feel a mix of positive and negative feelings at the same time, like being excited but also nervous, or happy but unsure about what will happen next. For example, you might feel excited about a big school performance, but also nervous because you're unsure how it will turn out. These mixed feelings are normal and can happen when you're facing something new or uncertain! Have you ever felt like this?"

Minty: "Sometimes, our feelings are triggered by certain things called **TRIGGERS.** For example, if someone says something hurtful or does something you don't like, you might feel angry. Or, if you're about to speak in front of the class, you might feel nervous or excited. But remember, each person may feel and react in their own way. It's important to understand this and act accordingly."

Can you match these feelings with the emojis below?

Scared	
Relaxed	
Angry	
Shocked	
Tensed	

- When we experience emotions, our bodies also react. For example, when we're excited or nervous, our heart rate may increase, and we might start sweating. When we're scared or anxious, our hands might get cold, or we could feel a tightness in our chest.

- If you're feeling negative emotions, there are many ways to clear them. For example, talking about your feelings with someone, doing creative activities like drawing, writing, or music/dance, or engaging in physical activities like sports, walking, or cycling.

- When you're feeling angry, you can try tricks like counting to ten, squeezing a stress ball, or practicing deep breathing.

- If you're feeling jealous, take a moment to think about the things you do well and be thankful for them. Doing something kind for others can also help you feel good about yourself.

Minty: "Everyone experiences different types of feelings, and that's completely natural. Even if you have negative feelings, don't try to suppress them—just release them. Talk to your parents or friends about how you're feeling. Did you like what Aunt Ziva taught me?"

Minty: "Alright, see you next time!"

Hope Minty made the concept of feelings clear for you! Now, here's a wonderful activity to brighten your day. It's important to understand your strengths to feel good about yourself. Fill in the strength chart given in next page!

MY STRENGTH CHART

My Top 5 Strengths are:

1. _______________________________

2. _______________________________

3. _______________________________

4. _______________________________

5. _______________________________

I have many other strengths that I am working on and improving:

6. Understanding My Boundaries

Minty: "Hello friends! Today, I have my younger siblings with me, and I'm taking them to a pool party. Say 'Hi' to them!"

____

____

Minty: "This is their new pair of bathing suits that Mom bought for them. Do you know that the parts covered under a bathing suit are called private parts? Can you recall what the private parts of boys and girls are?"

____

____

Minty: "Yes, for boys, it's the penis and buttocks. For girls, it's the chest, vulva, and buttocks. In addition, the lips are also considered a private part. _Private_ means these parts are for you only and are not meant to be shared with others. Here's a _Private Parts Rule Book_:"

PRIVATE PARTS RULE BOOK

- You should not show your private parts to anyone.

- You should not let anyone touch your private parts.

- You should not let anyone photograph your private parts.

- You should not see, touch, or photograph anyone else's private parts.

- You should not watch photos or videos of anyone's private parts.

- You should not look, touch, or photograph even if someone shows theirs to you.

Minty: "Remember, if anyone tries to touch or photograph your private parts, you should say **"NO," "GET AWAY," and "TELL"** a trusted adult. If they don't listen, keep telling them until they believe you. If one person doesn't believe you, tell another trusted adult until you find someone who does. Do you know what these kinds of touches are called?"

____

____

Minty: "Yes, these kinds of touches are called *bad touches.* I will explain more about them, but first, let's look at the pictures given here. These touches make you feel happy, safe, and comfortable. These are known as *good touches.* Now, can you draw emojis in the table below to show how these touches feel?"

HOW GOOD TOUCHES FEEL:

Minty: "Brilliant! Touches that hurt, make you feel scared, angry, confused, or ashamed are bad touches. Recall that any touch related to your private parts is also a bad touch. Remember, what should you do when someone touches or tries to touch there?"

____

____

Draw emojis in the table below to show how bad touches feel.

HOW BAD TOUCHES FEEL:

Minty: "Exactly! If someone touches you badly, you should say **"NO," "GET AWAY," and "TELL."** See, when you are a child or if you have any illness or disability that prevents you from bathing or dressing on your own, you can get help from your parents or caretakers. During these times, they may need to help you apply medicine or assist you with other things. In these situations, your parents or guardians may see or touch your private parts, but it should always make you feel safe. If it doesn't, that's not good. A doctor or nurse may also need to see or touch your private parts to treat or check you, but only in the presence of your parents. Also, remember it is important to tell a trusted adult when bad touch happens. But do you know whom should you tell?"

____

____

Minty: "A trusted adult is someone over 18 years old who makes you feel safe and comfortable. You can tell them anything, and they won't abandon you. They will help keep you safe and protected. Here are some examples:"

Minty: "It's always a good idea to list your trusted adults' names and phone numbers and keep it with you. You can even memorize these things. Fill in the blanks below with your trusted adults' details. While you do that, let me have some playtime!"

Minty gave you a great activity to complete, and I hope you understand its importance. Keep it with you so that you can refer to it whenever needed. Here's something else you should remember:

Privacy:

Understanding privacy is just as important as understanding private parts. ***Privacy*** means being away from others. There are certain things we do that we want to keep private, like bathing, changing clothes, or using the toilet. That's our personal space, and nobody should peek into it, nor should we peek into others' private moments. Similarly, our parents also have their privacy. If two adults want to spend time together, it's their choice. We should not intrude into that.

Body Boundaries:

Body Boundaries are equally important. Everyone has certain boundaries, especially with people who are not close or familiar. While talking or interacting, it's essential to maintain personal space as a good manner. We should establish strong boundaries. If anyone tries to break them, you should say ***STOP.***

7. Keeping My Body Safe

Minty: "Hey friends! How are your classes going?"

____

____

Minty: "Yesterday in my class, a lady named Isha came to give a session on abuse prevention. Do you know what abuse means?"

____

____

Minty: "Abuse means mistreatment or harm done to someone, and it can happen in different forms like physical, emotional, and sexual. Here's a brief description of each:"

- **Physical abuse**: Hurting someone's body, like hitting or kicking.

- **Emotional abuse**: Saying or doing things that make someone feel bad about themselves, like calling them hurtful names, making fun of them, or saying mean things to make them sad.

- **Sexual abuse**: Touching someone in a way that makes them uncomfortable or that they didn't agree to, especially in private parts of their body.

Minty: "Remember, touching private parts like your penis, vulva, lips, chest, or buttocks in an inappropriate way is considered a bad touch and is a part of abuse. Look at the picture below:"

Minty: "Yes, in the picture, parts marked in red and yellow are areas where it's not okay to be touched, while green areas are safe to touch. If someone abuses you, you may feel negative emotions, but it's important to know that it is not your fault. It's never because of anything you did. The person who touched you badly is the one in the wrong. You should always report such incidents to a trusted adult. Now, let me ask you a question. Who do you think could be an abuser? Is it someone you don't know? Can you describe them?"

Minty: "Anyone can be an abuser. Sometimes, they may be older or more powerful than you. They can be a man or a woman, and they could be someone you know or don't know. So, how can you tell if someone is a safe stranger or an unsafe stranger?"

Minty: "Here are some tips to help you identify safe and unsafe strangers. Refer to the table on the next page."

Safe Strangers	Unsafe Strangers
They keep a proper distance and don't touch you.	They try to touch you in ways that make you uncomfortable.
They talk nicely and don't make you feel scared.	They ask you to keep secrets, especially about touching or gifts.
They don't ask you to keep secrets or give gifts without a reason.	They try to take you to a private place or be alone with you.
They don't ask personal questions about your body or family.	They ask strange questions about your body or family.
They don't try to be alone with you.	They behave in a way that scares, confuses, or pressures you.
Their behavior is steady and doesn't suddenly change.	Their behavior changes suddenly, like being too friendly or too pushy.
	They make you feel uneasy, even if they seem nice.

Minty: "Hey! I wonder, who is at more risk of abuse? Boys or girls?"

____

____

Minty: "The truth is, everyone is at risk for abuse. So, don't think you're immune to it. But don't panic. I have some tips to help you stay safe while interacting with strangers:"

TIPS TO STAY SAFE

1. **Never go anywhere with a stranger**: Always stay close to your trusted adults and never agree to leave with someone you don't know, even if they seem nice.

2. **Never be alone in a closed space with a stranger**: Always ensure you're in a public or visible area if a stranger is around.

3. **Never share your personal details with strangers**: Whether online or offline, don't reveal personal information like your name, address, or phone number to someone you don't trust.

4. **Never keep secrets or secret gifts from a stranger**: If a stranger gives you something or asks you to keep it a secret, tell your parents or a trusted adult immediately. (Remember, secrets are not okay to keep even if from known persons)

5. **Be cautious of strangers who act overly caring or generous**: Some people with bad intentions may try to gain your trust by being overly nice. Always trust your instincts and stay alert.

Minty: "I'm glad you're interested in these topics. I'm sure the knowledge you gain will help you stay strong and safe as you grow up!"

8. Online Safety

Minty: "Hi, friends! Today, my older brother, Beyon, got a new phone. It's amazing! We took some family photos, too. It has the LUDO app on it, and I love playing it. Do you use mobile phones?"

____

____

Minty: "Okay… Even though mobile phones aren't made for kids, they can be helpful for learning new things, listening to music, and playing games. However, we should only use them with adults' guidance. Spending too much time on screens can also be harmful in many ways. Do you use the internet on your phone? If yes, what do you do on the internet?"

____

____

Minty: My brother told me there are certain rules to follow when using the internet, especially on platforms like Instagram, WhatsApp, and Facebook. Have you heard of these rules? What are they?

____

____

Minty: "Okay! I'll share what I learned. Look at the table here:"

Sl. No.	Online Safety Rules	Description
1	Ask Before You Go Online	Always get permission from your parents or guardians before using the internet. This helps them guide you to safe websites and apps.
2	Keep Personal Information Private	Never share your name, address, phone number, school name, passwords, or photos online. Personal details can be misused by strangers.
3	Be Cautious with Strangers Online	Don't talk to or share information with people you don't know. Strangers online might pretend to be someone they're not.
4	Create Strong Passwords	Use a mix of letters, numbers, and symbols in your passwords, and never share them with anyone—not even friends. But is good to share it with your parents. Strong passwords protect your accounts.
5	Think Before You Upload Photos and Videos	Whatever you post online stays forever, even if you delete it. Avoid sharing anything that might hurt you or others later.
6	Avoid Clicking on Unknown Links	Suspicious links or pop-ups can have harmful software (viruses) or trick you into sharing private information.
7	Say No to Secret Conversations	If someone asks you to keep online chats or activities secret, tell a trusted adult. Secrets online can be dangerous.
8	Report Anything That Feels Wrong	If something online makes you feel upset, scared, or uncomfortable, inform a parent, teacher, or trusted adult immediately.

9	Stick to Safe Platforms	Use apps, websites, and games that are made for kids your age. Check if your parents approve them first.
10	Balance Screen Time	Too much screen time can affect your health, like your eyes, sleep, and mood. Take breaks and enjoy other activities like playing outdoors or reading.
11	Avoid Using Public Wi-Fi Without Supervision	Public networks can be unsafe. Only use them with a parent's guidance.
12	Check for HTTPS	Before entering any information, ensure the website starts with "https://" It shows the site is secure.
13	Be Aware of Fake Profiles	People can pretend to be kids online. Always verify with your parents if someone seems suspicious.
14	Know About Cyberbullying	If someone is mean to you or others online, don't respond. Save evidence and report it to a trusted adult.

Minty: "I hope these rules help you a lot! I have a fun game for you to try. Come and check it out!"

CROSSWORD PUZZLE

ACROSS

3. The act of sending hurtful messages or spreading rumors about someone online.

5. A made-up identification used to trick others online.

6. A secret code that protects your online accounts from being accessed by others.

DOWN

1. A technology that allows you to connect to the internet wirelessly.

2. You need this from a parent or guardian before using the internet.

4. The secure version of a website's address that protects your data when browsing.

9. My Smart Safety Plan

Minty: "Hi friends! Yesterday, something very important happened to my friend's younger sister, Alena. She went to a church with her family and got lost in the crowd. Alena is just 6 years old, but she did something amazing! She spotted a policeman (a safe stranger) and told him she was lost. Alena knew her parents' phone number and their full names. The policeman quickly helped her find her family. Have you ever experienced something like this?"

____

____

Minty: "Alena's smartness is truly inspiring! It's so important to know whom to ask for help when you're in trouble. Always remember these lessons so you can stay safe too!"

WHOM TO ASK FOR HELP:

- Always talk to trusted adults like parents, teachers, or family friends if you feel unsafe.
- Uniformed helpers like police, firefighters, or security guards are trained to help in emergencies.
- Shopkeepers, librarians, or workers in public places are safer to approach because they are often in public areas where others can see them and are likely to help responsibly.
- Adults with kids are usually safe to ask for help if you're lost or scared.

Minty: "It's also very important to memorize certain details! I've made a simple checklist for you. Once you've memorized them, tick them off:"

Sl.No.	Items	Status
1	Memorize your parents' full name and phone numbers.	☐
2	Memorize your home address and school address.	☐
3	Write down important phone numbers and keep them in an easy-to-access spot. (Eg: Inside your pencil box)	☐
4	Learn and remember your family's code word for emergencies. (Note: Always ask for the code word before opening the door when home alone.)	☐

Emergency Information Sheet

Fill in the details below so you can easily access them when needed:

- **Mother's Name & Phone Number**: ___________________________________

- **Father's Name & Phone Number**: ___________________________________

- **Trusted Neighbor's Name & Phone Number**: ___________________________

- **Home Address**: ___________________________________

- **School Address**: ___________________________________

- **Child Helpline: 1098** (You can also memorize this number and they will help you when in trouble)

Minty: "Did you fill out the emergency information sheet? That's great! Now, it's also important to remember safe places to go when you feel unsafe. Learn about safe spots in your area, like hospitals, schools, or stores. These places have systems to help in emergencies and are good places to go if you're feeling unsafe. You can also stay in public places like playgrounds, malls, or libraries. Being in populated areas increases your safety because there are many people around who can help you."

Minty: "Do you know what to do if a stranger enters your house and you feel unsafe?"

Minty: "It's important to know how to exit your house quickly through the front or back door, and make sure the escape routes are clear and safe. Practice using them with your family. Keep your keys in a place where you can access them in case of an emergency. If someone is making you feel unsafe or uncomfortable, leave immediately and go to a trusted neighbor's house or a public place. Finally, here are some do's and don'ts to keep you safe:"

THINGS THAT ARE NOT OKAY TO DO	THINGS THAT ARE OKAY TO DO
Don't go anywhere with someone you don't know.	Immediately say STOP or YELL when someone makes you feel unsafe or touches you inappropriately.
Don't go anywhere with someone who makes you feel uneasy, even if they say they were sent by your parents.	Immediately GET AWAY from an unsafe space.
Don't keep secrets, especially if it is about touch (e.g., touching private parts).	Learn safe places to go.
Don't accept gifts from strangers.	Learn to identify safe strangers.
Don't accept gifts from someone you know if they ask you to keep the gift a secret.	Identify trusted adults to approach when in danger.
Don't open the door to anyone when you are home alone, unless they know your family's code word.	Let your parents know if a stranger is being overly friendly with you.
Don't be in a closed space with a stranger.	If you feel unsafe outside, stay in a crowded area like a store, library, or park.
Don't panic when you feel unsafe.	Report to an adult when you feel unsafe.

Minty: "You might have questions about what you've learned in this book. Do you know who to ask your doubts?

____

____

Minty: "If you ever have any doubts or concerns, remember to talk to a trusted adult. This could be a parent, teacher, or a family member who cares about you and wants to keep you safe. They are always there to help. And if you need urgent assistance, you can call the child helpline at 1098. That's all for today. See you again soon!"

10. Roleplays

Minty: "Hey friends, we have come to the end of this beautiful journey. I have brought you a very interesting game in this last chapter. Here are five imaginary scenarios with fictional characters. Just read through them and answer the questions based on the knowledge you've gained from this book. Ready? Let's get started!"

SCENARIO 1

Roy was playing in his front yard when a man drove up in a car and waved at him. "Hi there, your dad sent me to pick you up. I'm taking you to his work. He said it's okay," the man said. Roy felt unsure because he didn't recognize the man. Roy remembered what his parents told him and said, "No, thank you!" He ran inside and told his grandparents right away.

1 What should Roy do when he doesn't recognize the man?

A) Go with the man

B) Politely say no and run inside to tell his grand parents

C) Stay quiet and wait to see what happens

2 Why is it important for Roy to tell his grand parents about the situation?

A) So they can help keep him safe

B) So they can give him permission to leave

C) So they don't worry about him

3   Why did Roy decide not to go with the man?

    A)   He didn't recognize the man and felt unsure.

    B)   The man didn't have candy.

    C)   Roy didn't feel like going out.

SCENARIO TWO

    Anaya was at her cousin's house when her older cousin, **Sami**, showed her a magazine with pictures of people without clothes. Anaya felt uncomfortable and told Sami, "I don't want to look at that." Sami laughed and said, "It's just for fun, don't tell anyone!" Anaya left the room and told her mom immediately.

---

1   What should Anaya do when her cousin shows her inappropriate pictures?

    A)   Laugh and pretend it's funny

    B)   Tell her cousin to stop and leave the room

    C)   Keep the secret and not tell anyone

2   Why is it important for Anaya to tell her mom what happened?

    A)   So her cousin doesn't get upset

    B)   So her mom doesn't feel sad

    C)   So her mom can help explain what's right and safe

3   What is the best way for Anaya to handle similar situations in the future?

   A)   Ignore it and hope it stops

   B)   Tell a trusted adult immediately if something makes her uncomfortable

   C)   Keep it to herself

SCENARIO THREE

Aaliya was at her parents' house when a family friend repeatedly came into the bathroom while she was taking a bath. Since the lock on the door was broken, she couldn't keep him out. Aaliya felt uncomfortable and, although she couldn't lock the door, she quickly finished her bath and decided to tell her parents about what had happened.

1   What should Aaliya do if the family friend keeps entering the bathroom while she's taking a bath?

   A)   Politely ask the family friend to leave the bathroom

   B)   Ignore the situation and stay silent

   C)   Tell her parents about what happened as soon as possible

2   Why did Aaliya feel uncomfortable when the family friend entered the bathroom?

    A)   She didn't want anyone to see her without clothes

    B)   The bathroom was too small

    C)   She didn't know how to lock the door

3   Why should others not enter the bathroom while someone is taking a bath or shower?

    A)   It's important to respect personal privacy

    B)   The bathroom is always open for anyone to use

    C)   People don't need permission to enter the bathroom

SCENARIO FOUR

Ibrahim was at the park when a stranger approached him and asked, "I'm looking for my dog. Can you help me find him?" Ibrahim politely said no and stayed near other people until his mom arrived to pick him up.

1   What should Ibrahim do when a stranger asks him for help?

    A)   Follow the stranger to help

    B)   Stay quiet and see what happens

    C)   Politely refuse and stay in a crowded area

2   Why is it safer for Ibrahim to stay in a crowded area?

   A)   There are more people who can help if something happens

   B)   He will get a chance to find the dog

   C)   He can leave the park if he's bored

3   What could Ibrahim do if the stranger insists on help?

   A)   Go with the stranger to be polite

   B)   Walk away and tell an adult immediately

   C)   Stay silent and avoid the situation

SCENARIO FIVE

Sania was at her uncle's house when he asked her to change her clothes in front of him. "You can't change in the bathroom. Let me help you with your clothes," he said. Sania felt uncomfortable and politely refused, saying, "I want to change in the bathroom." She then told her mom about it.

1   What should Sania do when her uncle asks her to change clothes in front of him?

   A)   Agree and change in front of him

   B)   Politely refuse and say she wants to change in the bathroom

   C)   Ignore him and change anyway

2   Why is it important for Sania to tell her mom what happened?

   A)   So her mom can help her stay safe

   B)   So her mom can buy her new clothes

   C)   So her uncle doesn't get upset

3   What should Sania do in the future if someone makes her feel uncomfortable?

   A)   Stay silent and hope it stops

   B)   Do whatever the person asks to avoid trouble

   C)   Trust her feelings and speak up to a trusted adult

Answer Key:

Scenario 1	Scenario 2	Scenario 3	Scenario 4	Scenario 5
B	B	C	C	B
A	C	A	A	A
A	B	A	B	C

Minty: "Great job, friends! You've completed the game, and I'm sure you're now even more confident in keeping yourself safe in different situations. Always remember, trust your instincts and talk to a trusted adult if something doesn't feel right. Keep learning and stay safe!"

"Now it's time for me to say goodbye, but don't feel sad! Remember, you can come back anytime you need to. I mentioned the MentX Super Squad at the beginning—it's a group of amazing people who know all about body safety rules and help others learn them too. I'm so happy I got to talk to you on behalf of my team. Always stay confident, safe, and brave."

"Wishing you all the very best!"

Epilogue

Hello, dear readers!

I hope you had as much fun with Minty as I did! It's completely natural to feel a little sad that our journey with Minty is coming to an end. But don't worry, you can always come back and visit her whenever you need! Minty would love to hear from you and share in your experiences. You can send her an email at:

mentxofficial@gmail.com

And here's something Minty promised—a special bonus! Turn to the next page to find your very own **MentX Super Squad Membership Card**! Once you've finished all the activities and readings in this book, fill out the card, and proudly display it on your study table. You've earned it!

For Parents:

Please help your child fill out the Membership Card and take a photo with it. Send it to us via email or share it on Instagram by tagging MentX. We'd love to spread this message to even more children, and your feedback helps us improve!

Thank you for your support, and let's continue spreading awareness and knowledge together!

<u>Super Squad Membership Card</u>

This is to certify that _______________________________

is an official member of the **MentX Super Squad!**

Age: ________

Date of Joining: _________________

Paste Your
Photo Here

My Body Safety Promise:
I promise to keep myself and others safe by remembering and sharing body safety rules. I will always speak up if I feel unsafe and help others learn how to stay safe too!

Super Squad Oath:

- I will always respect my own and others' boundaries.
- I will talk to a trusted adult if something makes me uncomfortable.
- I will help spread awareness about body safety to my friends and family.
- I am a proud member of the MentX Super Squad!

◆ **Signed by:** _______________________________ (Your name and signature)

◆ **Approved by:** Sandra K Anil (Founder of MentX)

References

1. Crime in India 2022 Statistics Volume 1.

2. Citak-Tunc G, et al. Preventing Child Sexual Abuse: Body Safety Training for Young Children in Turkey. J Child Sex Abus. 2018;27(4): DOI:10.1080/10538712.2018.1477001.

3. Miller-Perrin CL, Wurtele SK. Children's Conceptions of Personal Body Safety: A Comparison Across Ages. J Clin Child Psychol. 1989;18(1): DOI:10.1207/s15374424jccp1801_4.

4. Gerber N. Parent-Child Conversations about Body Safety and Consent. University of San Francisco Theses, Dissertations, Capstones and Projects. May 18, 2023.

5. UNESCO. International Technical Guidance on Sexuality Education.

6. Central Board of Secondary Education. Adolescence Education Programme. 2012.

7. Dr. Ankit Chandra. Complete Sex Education Guide.

www.ingramcontent.com/pod-product-compliance
Lightning Source LLC
Chambersburg PA
CBHW041642110726
48005CB00003B/688